C000270030

Taylor Swift Quiz Book

101 Questions To Test Your Knowledge Of This Incredibly Successful Musician

By Colin Carter

Taylor Swift Quiz

This book contains one hundred and one informative and entertaining trivia questions with multiple choice answers. With 101 questions, some easy, some more demanding, this entertaining book will really test your knowledge of Taylor Swift.

You will be quizzed on a wide range of topics associated with Taylor for you to test yourself; with questions on her early days, her songs, her lyrics, her achievements, her awards and much more, guaranteeing you a truly fun, educational experience.

This quiz book will provide entertainment for fans of all ages and will certainly test your knowledge of this world-famous musician. The book is packed with information and is a must-have for all true Taylor Swift fans, wherever you live in the world.

Published by Glowworm Press

glowwormpress.com

Disclaimer

ACKNOWLEDGEMENTS

My friend Miranda simply adores Taylor Swift.

As a writer, I thought I would write a book on Taylor for her to test himself and to see how much she really knows about the legend that is Taylor Swift.

Miranda told me that she was not alone, and that Taylor had millions of fans and that I should write the book for every one of them, not just her.

So that's what I have done!   This book is for all you wonderful Taylor Swift fans – wherever you live in the world.

I hope you enjoy it.

Colin Carter

Here is the first set of questions.

1. Which year was Taylor born?
   A. 1986
   B. 1987
   C. 1988
   D. 1989

2. What is Taylor's star sign?
   A. Aquarius
   B. Aries
   C. Leo
   D. Sagittarius

3. Where was Taylor born?
   A. California
   B. Georgia
   C. Pennsylvania
   D. Virginia

4. Where did she grow up?
   A. On a beach
   B. On a farm
   C. On an island
   D. On a yacht

5. What is Taylor's middle name?
   A. Abigail
   B. Alison
   C. Amber
   D. Ashley

6. Who is Taylor named after?
   A. Elizabeth Taylor
   B. James Taylor
   C. Lili Taylor
   D. Roger Taylor

7. What is the name of the book Taylor wrote when she was 14 years old?
   A. A Girl Named Girl
   B. Everything But The Girl
   C. Girl Power
   D. Once I Was A Girl

8. How tall is Taylor?
   A. 5 feet 4 inches
   B. 5 feet 6 inches
   C. 5 feet 8 inches
   D. 5 feet 10 inches

9. Which song did Taylor use to perfect her guitar playing?
   A. Adore Me

B. Hold Me
C. Kiss Me
D. Love Me

10. Which other instrument does Taylor play?
   A. Banjo
   B. Piano
   C. Ukulele
   D. All the above

Here are the answers to the first ten questions. If you get seven or more right, you are doing very well so far, but the questions will get harder.

A1. Taylor Swift was born on December 13th, 1989.

A2. Taylor's star sign is Sagittarius.

A3. Taylor Swift was born in West Reading, Pennsylvania.

A4. Swift had an unusual childhood, being brought up on a Christmas Tree Farm. She wrote a song about her experience on the 11 acre farm, aptly titled, "Christmas Tree Farm." The accompanying music video for the song featured clips from Taylor's childhood on the farm.

A5. Alison is Taylor's middle name.

A6. Taylor was named after singer-songwriter James Taylor, and her mother believed that if she had a gender-neutral name it would help her forge a business career. Swift's parents were also huge fans of James Taylor. A five-time

Grammy Award winner, he is one of the highest-selling music artists of all time, having sold more than 100 million records worldwide.

A7. When Taylor was 14 years old, she wrote a novel titled "A Girl Named Girl". It is about a mother who wanted a son instead of a girl. The book was never published but Taylor registered the trademark in 2020 to try and prevent anyone else using the title to cash in.

A8. Taylor is 5 feet 10 inches tall. In metric this is 1.8 metres.

A9. "Kiss Me" was the song Taylor used to help her learn guitar. She revealed in an interview with Vogue, that the 1997 hit by Sixpence None The Richer was the first song she played all the way through on her chosen instrument.

A10. Taylor is known for playing multiple instruments, including banjo, guitar (both acoustic and electric), piano and ukulele.

Here is the next set of questions.

11. What was the name of the record label that signed Taylor at the start of her music career?
    A. Atlantic Records
    B. Big Machine Records
    C. Columbia Records
    D. Warner Records

12. What is the title of Taylor's debut single that propelled her to fame?
    A. Love Story
    B. Our Song
    C. Teardrops on my Guitar
    D. Tim McGraw

13. What is the title of Taylor's debut album?
    A. I Am Taylor
    B. My Name Is Taylor
    C. Taylor Here
    D. Taylor Swift

14. When was Taylor's debut album released?
    A. 2002
    B. 2004
    C. 2006
    D. 2008

15. How many weeks was her debut album on the Billboard 200 chart?
    A. 127
    B. 137
    C. 147
    D. 157

16. What was Taylor's first number one single on the Billboard Hot 100 chart?
    A. Adore You
    B. Look What You Made Me Do
    C. Today Was A Fairytale
    D. We Are Never Ever Getting Back Together

17. What was the title of Taylor's debut solo tour?
    A. Fearless Tour
    B. The Red Tour
    C. Speak Now World Tour
    D. Taylor On Tour

18. What color eyes does Taylor have?
    A. Blue
    B. Brown
    C. Green
    D. Hazel

19. What was Taylor's first job before she pursued a career in music?
    A. Barista
    B. Computer programmer
    C. Waitress
    D. Web Designer

20. How many tattoos has Taylor got?
    A. 0
    B. 5
    C. 10
    D. 15

Here are the answers to the last set of questions.

A11. Taylor signed to Big Machine Records in 2005 when she started her music career. She was their first signed artist.

A12. Taylor's debut solo single was "Tim McGraw," which was released in June 2006. It is a powerful ballad that showcases her vocal range and song writing abilities.

A13. Taylor's debut album was simply entitled "Taylor Swift" which went on to be a huge success.

A14. Taylor's self-titled debut album "Taylor Swift" was released in October 2006.

A15. The "Taylor Swift" album spent an incredible 157 weeks on the Billboard 200 and registered more weeks on the chart than any other album in the whole of the 2000s decade.

A16. Taylor's first number one single in the US was "We Are Never Ever Getting Back Together" which topped the charts in 2012. Internationally, her first number one single in Australia was "Love Story" in 2008. In Canada her first number one single was "Today Was A Fairytale" in 2010. Taylor's career blossomed even later in the UK than elsewhere (her first UK hit came four years after her US debut) and her first official number one single in the UK was "Look What You Made Me Do" in 2017.

A17. Taylor's debut solo tour was titled "The Fearless Tour". It ran from April 2009 until July 2010 with over 100 shows including 52 shows in North America. Over a million people saw Taylor perform live during the tour, which showcased her incredible stage performances.

A18. Taylor's eye color is a piercing blue. A scientist has gone as far as saying they are electric blue with a tint of black.

A19. Taylor worked as a computer programmer before pursuing a career in music.

A20. Taylor does not have any permanent tattoos (to our knowledge), although she has dabbled with temporary tattoos.

Here is the next set of questions.

21. What is Taylor's official Instagram account?
    A. @taylorswift
    B. @taylorswiftlive
    C. @taylorswiftofficial
    D. @taylorswiftworld

22. What is the title of Taylor's second studio album?
    A. 1989
    B. Fearless
    C. Red
    D. Speak Now

23. Who is thought of as the inspiration behind the song "Bad Blood"?
    A. Beyoncé
    B. Katy Perry
    C. Lady Gaga
    D. Rihanna

24. Which music video features Taylor as a zombie?
    A. Bad Blood
    B. Blank Space
    C. I Don't Want To Live Forever
    D. Look What You Made Me Do

25. Which year did Taylor win her first Grammy award?
    A. 2008
    B. 2009
    C. 2010
    D. 2011

26. How old was Taylor when she had her first kiss?
    A. 14
    B. 15
    C. 16
    D. 17

27. What is the name of Taylor's third studio album?
    A. Speak Easy
    B. Speak Later
    C. Speak Now
    D. Speak Out

28. Which of these is a real song of Taylor's?
    A. Always Open
    B. Eyes Open
    C. Mind Open
    D. Wide Open

29. Which ex-member of One Direction briefly dated Taylor?
    A. Harry Styles
    B. Liam Payne
    C. Louis Tomlinson
    D. Niall Horan

30. What was the name of the record label that Taylor moved to in 2018?
    A. Island Records
    B. RCA Records
    C. Republic Records
    D. Virgin Records

Here are the answers to the last block of questions.

A21. @taylorswift is the official Instagram account. It is one of the most followed Instagram accounts. A number of her Instagram posts have had over 10 million likes!

A22. Taylor's second studio album, released in 2008, is "Fearless." The album received critical acclaim and commercial success, further establishing Taylor's artistic identity. It is the most awarded album in country music history, including winning Album of the Year at the Grammy Awards in 2010.

A23. It is widely reported that "Bad Blood" was written about Taylor's well publicized feud with Katy Perry.

A24. The music video featuring Taylor as a zombie is "Look What You Made Me Do." It really is worth watching on YouTube.

A25. In 2010, Taylor won her first Grammy award. In fact, she won FOUR Grammy awards – including two awards for "Fearless." Not bad for a 20-year-old!

A26. Taylor's first kiss was with her first boyfriend at the age of 15. She said, "I was one of the last of my friends to ever kiss a guy. It wasn't a bad kiss. I think it was cute. We ended up dating for a year."

A27. Taylor's third studio album is called "Speak Now." It was released in October 2010.

A28. "Eyes Open" was a single Taylor released in March 2012. The song garnered critical acclaim with critics favorably noting the song's more rock-oriented tone as compared to her previous releases.

A29. Harry Styles briefly dated Taylor. The pair met in 2012 when Taylor was 22 and Harry was 18 and they dated for a few months.

A30. Taylor moved to Republic Records in November 2018 after her contract with Big Machine Records expired. There had been underlying friction for a while and in June 2019, she came into dispute with Big Machine Records over the ownership of the masters of her first six studio albums. These albums were later re-mixed and released as Taylor's versions.

Here is the next set of questions.

31. What is the title of Taylor Swift's first live album?
    A. Folklore: The Long Pond Studio Sessions
    B. Live From Clear Channel Stripped
    C. Lover (Live From Paris)
    D. Speak Now World Tour - Live

32. Which music video features Taylor as a cyborg in a futuristic world?
    A. Delicate
    B. End Game
    C. I Don't Wanna Live Forever
    D. Ready For It?

33. Which album includes the songs "All Too Well" and "I Knew You Were Trouble"?
    A. Lover
    B. Red
    C. Reputation
    D. Speak Now

34. What is the title of Taylor's 2019 album that was her first after quitting Big Machine Records?
    A. Fearless
    B. Folklore

C. Lover

D. Red

35. What album includes the songs "Love Story" and "You Belong with Me"?
    A. 1989
    B. Fearless
    C. Red
    D. Speak Now

36. What is the name of the 2020 album that Taylor released during the COVID-19 pandemic?
    A. Evermore
    B. Folklore
    C. Reputation
    D. Midnights

37. Which album includes the hit songs "Shake It Off" and "Blank Space"?
    A. 1989
    B. Lover
    C. Reputation
    D. Speak Now

38. Who was credited as co-writing "Shake It Off"?
    A. Ed Sheeran
    B. Jack Antonoff

C. Kendrick Lamar

D. Max Martin

39. What is the title of the Netflix documentary film on Taylor released in 2020?

    A. Miss Adventure
    B. Miss Americana
    C. Miss Fortune
    D. Miss Understood

40. In which music video did Taylor transform into a male character named 'Tyler'?

    A. Look What You Made Me Do
    B. Me!
    C. The Man
    D. You Belong With Me

Here is the latest set of answers.

A31. The title of Taylor's first live album, released in November 2011, is "Speak Now World Tour - Live."

A32. Taylor appears as a cyborg in the music video for "Ready For It?" The video has a futuristic vibe featuring her as a replicant / human robot cyborg.

A33. The album that includes the songs "All Too Well" and "I Knew You Were Trouble" is "Red."

A34. The title of Taylor's 2019 album; her first album after her departure from Big Machine Records, is "Lover." Taylor conceived the album as a "love letter to love", taking inspiration from her revitalized personal life at the time.

A35. "Fearless " includes the songs "Love Story" and "You Belong with Me."

A36. This is a little bit of a trick question. In July 2020 Taylor released "Folklore" and in December 2020 she released "Evermore." Give yourself a bonus point if you knew that. No more trick questions, I promise.

A37. The album that includes the hit songs "Shake It Off" and "Blank Space" is "1989." The album was titled after Taylor's year of birth. The album also features the songs "Bad Blood" and "Style."

A38. "Shake It Off" was co-written by Taylor Swift and Max Martin, among others.

A39. "Miss Americana" is the title of the documentary film on Taylor released on Netflix in 2020.

A40. Taylor transformed into a male character dubbed 'Tyler' in the music video for "The Man." The song revolves around the idea that she wouldn't have to deal with petty stereotypes if she were a man.

Let's have some lyric related questions.

41. Which song starts with the lyrics, "You said the way my blue eyes shined put those Georgia stars to shame that night"?
   A. Lavender Haze
   B. Love Story
   C. The Story Of Us
   D. Tim McGraw

42. Which song starts with the lyrics, "We could leave the Christmas lights up 'til January"?
   A. Lover
   B. Red
   C. Today Was A Fairytale
   D. You Belong With Me

43. Which song contains the lyrics, "I have this thing where I get older but just never wiser"?
   A. Anti-Hero
   B. Delicate
   C. Our Song
   D. Wildest Dreams

44. Which song contains the lyrics, "I got a list of names, and yours is in red, underlined"?
   A. Bad Blood

B. End Game
C. Look What You Made Me Do
D. Style

45. Which song contains the lyrics, "Let's get out of this town, drive out of the city, away from the crowds"?
    A. Back To December
    B. Begin Again
    C. Getaway Car
    D. Wildest Dreams

46. Which song contains the lyrics, "Cause baby I could build a castle out of all the bricks they threw at me"?
    A. Blank Space
    B. New Romantics
    C. Ours
    D. Ready For It?

47. Which song contains the lyrics, "You call me up again just to break me like a promise"?
    A. All Too Well
    B. Fifteen
    C. Our Song
    D. The Last Time

48. Which song contains the lyrics, "We can't make any promises now can we, babe? But you can make me a drink"?
    A. Blank Space
    B. Delicate
    C. Shake It Off
    D. Style

49. Which song contains the lyrics, "I'm like the water when your ship rolled in that night"?
    A. Everything Has Changed
    B. I Knew You Were Trouble
    C. Me!
    D. Willow

50. Which song contains the lyrics, "I'm damned if I do give a damn what people say"?
    A. I Don't Want To Live Forever
    B. Lavender Haze
    C. Out of the Woods
    D. You Need To Calm Down

Here are the answers to the lyrics related questions.

A41. The lyrics "You said the way my blue eyes shined put those Georgia stars to shame that night" are the opening lines to "Tim McGraw," Taylor's debut single.

A42. The lyrics "We could leave the Christmas lights up 'til January" is the opening line to "Lover," where Taylor sings about the idea of leaving Christmas lights up as a symbol of enduring love.

A43. "I have this thing where I get older but just never wiser" is the opening line to Taylor's smash hit "Anti-Hero".

A44. The lyrics "I got a list of names, and yours is in red, underlined" are from "Look What You Made Me Do."

A45. The lyrics "He said, 'Let's get out of this town, drive out of the city, away from the crowds'" are from "Wildest Dreams," where Taylor sings about a desire for escape and adventure with a special someone.

A46. The lyrics "Cause baby I could build a castle out of all the bricks they threw at me" are from "New Romantics," a song which addresses the nonchalant and whimsical nature of the way young adults approach love.

A47. The lyrics "You call me up again just to break me like a promise" are from "All Too Well," a song known for its emotional depth and storytelling about a past relationship.

A48. The lyrics "We can't make any promises, now can we, babe? but you can make me a drink" are from "Delicate," where Taylor sings about the uncertainties of a new relationship.

A49. The lyrics "I'm like the water when your ship rolled in that night" is the opening line to "Willow". Taylor explained the song's meaning to be about wanting someone, the start of falling in love.

A50. "Lavender Haze" features the lyrics "I'm damned if I do give a damn what people say".

Here is the next set of questions.

51. What is Taylor's official X (aka twitter) account?
    A. @taylorswift
    B. @taylorswift3
    C. @taylorswift13
    D. @taylorswift23

52. What was the first single released from the album "1989"?
    A. Bad Blood
    B. Blank Space
    C. Shake It Off
    D. Style

53. In which film did Taylor voice the character Audrey in 2012?
    A. Frozen
    B. Moana
    C. The Lorax
    D. Zootopia

54. Which musician co-wrote the song "Breathe"?
    A. Natasha Bedingfield
    B. Colbie Caillat
    C. Kelly Clarkson
    D. Carrie Underwood

55. Which actor starred as Taylor's love interest in the music video for "Wildest Dreams"?
    A. Scott Eastwood
    B. Zac Efron
    C. Chris Hemsworth
    D. Tom Hiddleston

56. What album features the songs "Ours" and "Back to December"?
    A. Evermore
    B. Folklore
    C. Reputation
    D. Speak Now

57. What is Taylor's favorite TV show?
    A. Friends
    B. Game Of Thrones
    C. Greys Anatomy
    D. The Traitors

58. Which of Taylor's songs was inspired by the life of Rebekah Harkness?
    A. August
    B. Betty
    C. Cardigan
    D. The Last Great American Dynasty

59. What is the name of Taylor's philanthropic initiative aimed at helping those affected by natural disasters?
    A. Swift Aid
    B. Swift Help
    C. Swift Hope
    D. Swift Relief

60. Which album was primarily inspired by Taylor's experiences during high school?
    A. 1989
    B. Fearless
    C. Red
    D. Speak Now

Here goes with the latest set of answers.

A51. @taylorswift13 is the official X aka twitter account. It was set up in December 2008 and it has over 100 million followers.

A52. The lead single from the "1989" album was "Shake It Off" which was released in August 2014 and went onto be a hugely successful single.

A53. Taylor voiced the character Audrey in the film "The Lorax" in 2012.

A54. Colbie Caillat co-wrote "Breathe" with Taylor. It featured on the album "Fearless," and was later re-recorded for "Fearless (Taylor's version)."

A55. Scott Eastwood, Clint's son, appeared alongside Taylor in the music video for "Wildest Dreams."

A56. The album that features the songs "Ours" and "Back to December" is "Speak Now."

A57. Taylor's favorite TV show is either Friends or Grey's Anatomy, depending upon your source. She named one of her cats

Meredith after Ellen Pompeo's character on the medical drama show and she has tweeted many times about how much she loves watching the show. She has also publicly stated that Friends is her favorite TV show ever. Give yourself a point for either answer.

A58. The song inspired by the life of Rebekah Harkness is "The Last Great American Dynasty."

A59. The name of Taylor's philanthropic initiative aimed at helping those affected by natural disasters is "Swift Aid."

A60. "Fearless" is the album that was primarily inspired by Taylor's experiences during high school.

Hope you're having fun. Here is the next set of questions.

61. What is Taylor's highest selling song ever?
    A. Anti-Hero
    B. Blank Space
    C. Shake It Off
    D. You Belong With Me

62. What is the title of Taylor's song that references her ongoing feud with Kanye West?
    A. Bad Blood
    B. Blank Space
    C. Shake It Off
    D. This Is Why We Can't Have Nice Things

63. What is the name of Taylor's brother?
    A. Austin
    B. Brad
    C. Carter
    D. Mason

64. How many subscribers are there to the official Taylor Swift YouTube channel?
    A. 5 million
    B. 15 million
    C. 35 million

D. 55 million

65. In which music video does Taylor play the role of Juliet from Shakespeare's "Romeo and Juliet"?
    A. Love Story
    B. Mine
    C. White Horse
    D. You Belong with Me

66. What is the title of Taylor's song that pays tribute to her mother's battle with cancer?
    A. Change
    B. Exile
    C. Innocent
    D. Soon You'll Get Better

67. Who is the co-writer of Taylor's hit "Love Story"?
    A. Jack Antonoff
    B. Joe Alwyn
    C. Max Martin
    D. Nathan Chapman

68. What is Taylor's official website address?
    A. taylorswift.com
    B. taylorswift13.com
    C. taylorofficial.com
    D. officialtaylorswift.com

69. Which album features the songs "Karma" and "Lavender Haze"?
    A. Evermore
    B. Folklore
    C. Lover
    D. Midnights

70. Which of these songs did Taylor write for the soundtrack of "The Hunger Games"?
    A. Eyes Open
    B. Safe & Sound
    C. The Archer
    D. White Horse

Here is the latest set of answers.

A61. "Shake It Off" is widely regarded as Taylor's top-selling song ever. It has sold 3 million copies in the UK alone.

A62. "Innocent" is a song which was inspired by the dramatic confrontation Taylor experienced with rapper Kanye West at the 2009 MTV VMAs. The title of Taylor's song that references her ongoing feud with West is "This Is Why We Can't Have Nice Things." The lyrics make Taylor's feelings clear.

A63. Taylor's brother is named Austin Swift and he refers to her by his pet name 'Teffy'!

A64. There are now over 55 million subscribers to Taylor's YouTube Channel. Hopefully, you're one of them!

A65. Taylor plays the role of Juliet from Shakespeare's "Romeo and Juliet" in the music video for "Love Story."

A66.The title of Taylor's song that pays tribute to her mother's battle with cancer is "Soon You'll Get Better."

A67. Nathan Chapman is the co-writer of the hit song "Love Story."

A68. taylorswift.com is the official website. It provides a wealth of information including all the latest news, historical material, a complete discography and of course merch.

A69. The album that features the songs "Karma" and "Lavender Haze" is "Midnights" which was released in October 2022. The album also includes "Anti-Hero."

A70. Taylor actually wrote two songs for the soundtrack of "The Hunger Games: Songs from District 12 and Beyond." The two songs were "Safe & Sound" and "Eyes Open" although the latter was not included in the film itself. Give yourself a bonus point if you knew that.

Let's have some opening line questions.

71. Which song begins with the lyrics, "I remember when we broke up, the first time"?
    A. Fearless
    B. Teardrops on my Guitar
    C. We Are Never Ever Getting Back Together
    D. White Horse

72. Which song begins with the lyrics, "You're talking shit for the hell of it"?
    A. End Game
    B. Karma
    C. Maroon
    D. Picture To Burn

73. Which song begins with the lyrics, "I'm so glad you made time to see me. How's life? Tell me, how's your family"?
    A. Back to December
    B. Betty
    C. Look What You Made Me Do
    D. You Belong with Me

74. Which song begins with the lyrics, "It's strange to think the songs we used to sing,

the smiles, the flowers, everything is gone"?
- A. Bad Blood
- B. Exile
- C. Ready For It?
- D. Should've Said No

75. Which song begins with the lyrics, "Once upon a time, a few mistakes ago, I was in your sights, you got me alone"?
- A. Cardigan
- B. I Knew You Were Trouble
- C. Maroon
- D. You Need To Calm Down

76. Which song begins with the lyrics, "I stay out too late, got nothing in my brain. That's what people say"?
- A. Cruel Summer
- B. I Don't Want To Live Forever
- C. Shake It Off
- D. The Man

77. Which song begins with the lyrics, "State the obvious, I didn't get my perfect fantasy"?
- A. Mine
- B. Ours
- C. Picture To Burn

D. White Horse

78. Which song begins with the lyrics, "We were both young when I first saw you, I close my eyes and the flashback starts"?
    A. Exile
    B. Love Story
    C. Mean
    D. The Man

79. Which song begins with the lyrics, "There I was again tonight, forcing laughter, faking smiles"?
    A. Delicate
    B. Enchanted
    C. Mine
    D. Sparks Fly

80. Which song begins with the lyrics, "Fever dream high in the quiet of the night, you know that I caught it"?
    A. Begin Again
    B. Cruel Summer
    C. Style
    D. Today Was A Fairytale

Here are the answers to the opening lyrics section.

A71. "We Are Never Ever Getting Back Together," a song about moving on from a breakup, starts with the lyrics "I remember when we broke up, the first time."

A72. "Karma" starts with the lyrics "You're talking shit for the hell of it."

A73. The lyrics "I'm so glad you made time to see me. How's life? Tell me, how's your family" are the opening lines of "Back to December," where Taylor Swift reflects on past mistakes and missed opportunities in a relationship.

A74. The lyrics "It's strange to think the songs we used to sing, the smiles, the flowers, everything is gone" are the opening lines of "Should've Said No," a song about betrayal in a relationship.

A75. The lyrics "Once upon a time, a few mistakes ago, I was in your sights, you got me alone" are the opening lines of "I Knew You Were Trouble," a song about realizing the challenges in a relationship.

A76. The lyrics "I stay out too late, got nothing in my brain. That's what people say" are the opening lines of "Shake It Off," a song about realizing the challenges in a relationship.

A77. The lyrics "State the obvious, I didn't get my perfect fantasy" are the opening lines of "Picture To Burn," a song that features the banjo prominently.

A78. The lyrics "We were both young when I first saw you, I close my eyes and the flashback starts" are the opening lines of "Love Story," which is a modern-day Romeo and Juliet-inspired love story.

A79. The lyrics "There I was again tonight, forcing laughter, faking smiles" are from "Enchanted," where Taylor expresses the feeling of meeting someone special for the first time. It is a powerful ballad with acoustic guitar crescendos after each chorus.

A80. The lyrics "Fever dream high in the quiet of the night, you know that I caught it" are the opening lines to "Cruel Summer."

Here is the next set of questions.

81. What is the title of Taylor's song that serves as an anthem for standing up against bullying?
    A. Blank Space
    B. Change
    C. Innocent
    D. Mean

82. Which album features the songs "Mean" and "Mine"?
    A. Fearless
    B. Lover
    C. Red
    D. Speak Now

83. Which music video sees Taylor walking barefoot, surrounded by wolves that are hunting her?
    A. Bad Blood
    B. Blank Space
    C. Delicate
    D. Out of the Woods

84. What is the title of Taylor's song that features verses by Future and Ed Sheeran?
    A. Delicate
    B. End Game

C. Gorgeous

D. Look What You Made Me Do

85. What song mentions the movie star James Dean?

   A. August

   B. Betty

   C. Cardigan

   D. Style

86. What movie did Tayler feature in along with Jeff Bridges and Meryl Streep?

   A. The Gamer

   B. The Gazer

   C. The Giver

   D. The Gofer

87. Which album that features the songs "Teardrops on My Guitar" and "Should've Said No"?

   A. Fearless

   B. Lover

   C. Red

   D. Taylor Swift

88. Which song won Taylor the Best Music Video Award at the 2023 Grammy awards?

   A. A Place In This World

   B. All Too Well: The Short Film

C. The Lorax

D. The Real Taylor Swift: Wild Dreams

89. Which magazine declared Taylor as "Person of the Year" for 2023?

A. Billboard

B. NME

C. Rolling Stone

D. Time

90. Where was the music video for "Blank Space" mainly filmed?

A. Bulgaria

B. Italy

C. Spain

D. USA

Here is the latest set of answers.

A81. The title of Taylor's song that serves as an anthem for standing up against bullying is "Mean."

A82. The album that features the songs "Mean" and "Mine " is "Speak Now."

A83. Taylor is shown walking barefoot through a forest, surrounded by wolves that are hunting her, in the music video for "Out of the Woods."

A84. "End Game" features verses by Future and Ed Sheeran.

A85. In the song "Style" the lyrics "You got that James Dean daydream look in your eye" can be seen as a metaphor describing someone's appearance and demeanour. James Dean was an iconic actor from the 1950s who was known for his good looks and rebellious attitude. By using this reference, Taylor suggests that the person she is singing about has a similar cool and mysterious quality. As for who she is referring to, that is open to interpretation, but it is widely believed to be about her romance with Harry Styles.

A86. The Giver is a 2014 American 'social science fiction' film, based on the novel of the same name by Lois Lowry. The film starred Jeff Bridges, Meryl Streep, Katie Holmes, and of course Taylor Swift.

A87. The album that features the songs "Teardrops on My Guitar" and "Should've Said No" is "Taylor Swift." Other singles released from the album were "Our Song", "Picture To Burn" and of course "Tim McGraw" making it an incredibly productive debut album.

A88. At the 2023 Grammys Taylor won the Best Music Video category for "All Too Well: The Short Film." Well deserved it was too, as she wrote and directed the video, proving once again what an incredibly talented woman she is.

A89. Taylor was crowned Time Magazine's Person of The Year for 2023.

A90. The multi award-winning music video for "Blank Space" was mainly filmed at Oheka Castle in Long Island, New York.

Here goes with the final set of questions.

91. Which music video features elephants and zebras?
    A. Blank Space
    B. Out of the Woods
    C. Style
    D. Wildest Dreams

92. What is the title of Taylor's song that serves as a reflection on her childhood?
    A. Never Grow Up
    B. Out of the Woods
    C. Stay Stay Stay
    D. The Best Day

93. Who started dating Taylor in 2023?
    A. Travis Barker
    B. Travis Head
    C. Travis Kelce
    D. Travis Zajac

94. What is Taylor's most watched video on YouTube?
    A. Bad Blood
    B. Blank Space
    C. Shake It Off
    D. You Belong With Me

95. What is Taylor's favorite movie?
    A. Bridget Jones's Diary
    B. Four Weddings and a Funeral
    C. Love Actually
    D. Notting Hill

96. Which of these is a real song of Taylor's?
    A. 22
    B. 33
    C. 44
    D. 55

97. What is the name of Taylor's management company?
    A. 11 Management
    B. 13 Management
    C. 15 Management
    D. 17 Management

98. How many songs did Taylor write or co-write on her debut album?
    A. 3
    B. 5
    C. 7
    D. All of them

99. What is the name of Taylor's 2023 and 2024 concert tour?
    A. Reputation Stadium Tour

B. Speak Now Tour
C. The Eras Tour
D. The Taylor Tour

100.   How many Grammy awards has Taylor won?
    A. 7
    B. 9
    C. 11
    D. 13

101.   What is the name of Taylor Swift's fanbase?
    A. Swifties
    B. Swiftettes
    C. Swift Nation
    D. Stylers

Here is the final set of answers.

A91. A cheetah, elephants, a giraffe, a lion and zebras feature in the music video for "Wildest Dreams."

A92. The title of Taylor's song that serves as a reflection on her childhood and growing up is "Never Grow Up." She said, "It is a song about the fact that I don't quite know how I feel about growing up."

A93. In 2023, Taylor started dating American Football player Travis Kelce.

A94. "Shake It Off" takes the number one spot as the most watched Taylor Swift video on YouTube. It has had over 3 BILLION views.

A95. Taylor's favorite movie is 'Love Actually.' Amongst others it starred Hugh Grant, Colin Firth, Keira Knightley, Liam Neeson, Bill Nighy and Emma Thompson.

A96. "22" is a song that celebrates the feeling of being 22 years old: young, carefree, and in the mood to party and not think too much about life.

A97. Taylor's wholly-owned management company named 13 Management was established at the beginning of her career. Taylor was born on December 13 and has long proclaimed 13 as her favorite number. During her "Fearless" era, she wrote "13" on her guitar-strumming hand for good luck at her concerts and long-time fans often pay homage to that era by writing a "13" on their own hands.

A98. Taylor wrote or co-wrote every song on her debut album "Taylor Swift" showing that she was an early musical prodigy.

A99.The Eras Tour is the concert tour that Taylor started in March 2023 which involves her playing an incredible 146 shows across five continents over 20 months. She has described it as a journey through all of her musical "eras". The show is over three hours long, and the tickets sold out almost immediately. There is a supporting film called "Taylor Swift: The Eras Tour" which is incredible and is an absolute must-see.

A100. As at the end of March 2024, Taylor is the proud owner of 13 Grammy Awards. We are sure there are many more to come in the future.

A101. Taylor Swift's fanbase is affectionately known as "Swifties." Bet you already knew that!

That's a great question to finish with.

That's it. I hope you enjoyed this book, and I hope you got most of the answers right. I also hope you learnt some new things about this incredible woman!

If you have any comments or if you saw anything wrong, please email taylor@glowwormpress.com and we'll get the book updated.

Thanks for reading, and if you did enjoy the book, please leave a positive review on Amazon.

Printed in Great Britain
by Amazon

48268250R00036